Questions to Ask

Your Grandparents

ONE·FAM

www.onefam.com

Your Family Story

Founded in 2016, OneFam is the easy way to discover, preserve and relive your family history anywhere anytime. OneFam aims to make family history available to as many families as possible. Our suite of products include Journals, Family Tree Software (web, mobile and desktop), Ancestry DNA Testing and Family History Research. Connect, share and protect your family history for generations to come.

amazon.com

As a small company, we rely on your reviews to keep costs low for our customers and improve our products. Please spare a moment to rate or review this book on Amazon and share your experience with the Amazon community.

ONE FAM

Visit us at onefam.com

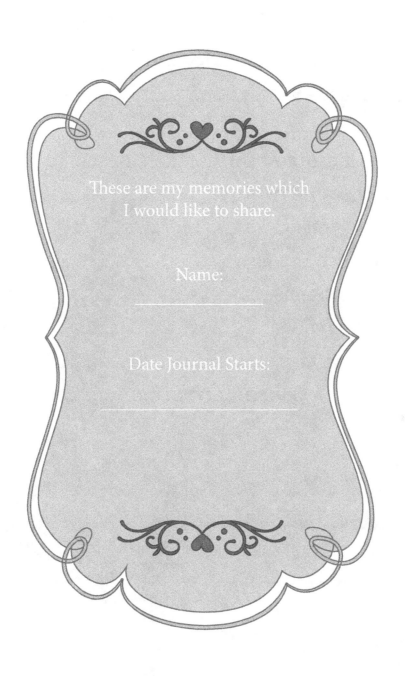

These are my memories which
I would like to share.

Name:

_____

Date Journal Starts:

_____

Table of Contents

Introduction

AsIsaidgoodbyetomyowngrandmotherathermemorialservice, themagnitudeofwhatwewerelosingfinallystruckme.Iwatchedthe hundredsofpeopleexpresstheircondolencestomyfamilyandtoshare theirexperiencesofmygrandmother.Thisquietwomanwastherock ofherfamilyandshedidnotevenknowit.Withoutherlife,noneof uswouldbeinthatroomcelebratingit.Infact,noneofuswouldbe thereatallhadshenotbeenthewife,mother,grandmotherandgreat grandmotherthatshewasofcourseandthesamegoesformygrandfather whohadpassedseveralyearsago.Hewasastrong,dependableandtall man.Ialwaysrememberedseeingthemtogether.Heandmygrandmother haddoneeverythingtogethersincetheyfirstmetatthetenderageofjust nineteenandstillholdinghandsalifetimelater.Whatwastheirsecret?

Lookingback,therearesomanythingsIdidn`tknowaboutthem.I shouldhavecapturedtheirfunnystoriesofgrowingupinasmall-town; theirjokesaboutmymomandhersiblingsasyoungchildren;thehilarious wordsthattheyhadstillused,wordswhichhadbeenlongforgottenbyour generation.

HadIrealizedthatsomedaytheywouldnolongerbehere,Iwouldhave askedsomanyquestions.Whathadtheirlifebeenlikegrowingup?How didtheymeet?Whydidtheymakethecareerchoicestheydidorhow didtheyviewtheworldoftoday?ThereIstood,realizingjusthowmany questionswereunansweredandthehundredsofmomentstocapturetheir stories, my story, lost to time.

Ishouldhaveaskedthemwhattheydreamedofdoingwiththeirlivesas youngsters?Whowastheirfavoritegrandchild(me,ofcourse)?Icould haveaskedhowtheyfeltaboutbeinggrandparents?ThenIwonder,what relationshipdidtheyhavewiththeirparentsorgrandparents?Whatwere even their names? Where did they come from?

But,Imissedoutonhavingthosememoriesforeverengravedinwriting. Iamcertaintheywouldhavelovedtosharesomuchmorewithmeand their future generations.

* * * * *

So, now there is a new grandparent in town....

Thisgrandparentisofanewgeneration;anew,"cooler"generation usingasmartphoneandgoingtoconcerts.Wewanttoshareour memorieswithourgrandchildren,allthedetails,rightdowntohowthey madeusfeelwhenwefirstlaideyesonthematthehospital.Willthey rememberthetripstotheparkwetookthemon,orwilltheyremember weweretheonewhotaughtthemtorideabike?Aboveall,willthey rememberourstory,ourhopesourdreams,ourlifeandhhowwelivedit.

Thisjournalismorethanjustawayofrecordingourmemories,itwillbe thelink,theconnectionbetweenthepastandthefuture.Itwillkeepthe conversationsbetweengenerationsaliveandthestoryofourfamily,our time, will never disappear from history.

Ihopeweallsharewithourgrandchildrentheunending,immeasurable feelingsofunbiasedlovethatwehaveforthemastheirgrandparents. Ihopetheywillpassonandsharethisinheritedlovewiththeirown childrenandgrandchildren.Sharingthroughourjournalwillinevitably leaveamarkonthisworldandcarryourlegacyonforgenerations.

Photograph

Why are you writing this story or autobiography?

_____

_____

_____

_____

_____

_____

_____

_____

_____

_____

What is it that you have always wanted to do in your life?

_____

_____

_____

_____

_____

_____

_____

_____

_____

_____

_____

_____

What do you expect to get out of telling your story?

_____

_____

_____

_____

_____

_____

_____

_____

_____

_____

Who are you writing this story for?

_____

_____

_____

_____

_____

_____

_____

_____

_____

_____

Who do you think will read your story/who is your audience?

_____
_____
_____
_____
_____
_____
_____
_____
_____

Was there a turning point in your life? A point when you decided to tell your story?

_____
_____
_____
_____
_____
_____
_____
_____
_____

Why do you feel it is important that people read/know your story?

_____

_____

_____

_____

_____

_____

_____

_____

_____

_____

Is there a message that you would like to share with your readers?

_____

_____

_____

_____

_____

_____

_____

_____

_____

_____

_____

What is your heritage?

_____

_____

_____

_____

_____

_____

_____

_____

_____

Where did your grandparents on both sides come from?

_____

_____

_____

_____

_____

_____

_____

_____

_____

Were they immigrants from another country?

_____

_____

_____

_____

_____

_____

_____

_____

_____

_____

Were they born into wealth or poverty?

_____

_____

_____

_____

_____

_____

_____

_____

_____

_____

_____

What level of education did they have?

How many siblings did they each have?

How did your grandparents meet?

_____

_____

_____

_____

_____

_____

_____

_____

_____

How many children did they have?

_____

_____

_____

_____

_____

_____

_____

_____

_____

What did they do for a living?

_____

_____

_____

_____

_____

_____

_____

_____

_____

When did they pass?

_____

_____

_____

_____

_____

_____

_____

_____

_____

_____

How did they pass away? At what age?

Did you know them?

If they are still living, how old are they?

_____

_____

_____

_____

_____

_____

_____

_____

Did you spend much time with them?

_____

_____

_____

_____

_____

_____

_____

_____

_____

What if any significant events were occurring in the world during their
lifetime?

_____

_____

_____

_____

_____

_____

_____

_____

_____

What do you remember most vividly about each of them?

_____

_____

_____

_____

_____

_____

_____

_____

_____

_____

Is there anything you wanted to ask them but never got a chance to?

Where were they born?

_____

_____

_____

_____

_____

_____

_____

_____

_____

How many siblings do they have?

_____

_____

_____

_____

_____

_____

_____

_____

_____

_____

Where do they fall in the birth order of the family?

_____

_____

_____

_____

_____

_____

_____

_____

_____

_____

What type of environment did each live in? Rural? Urban?

_____

_____

_____

_____

_____

_____

_____

_____

_____

_____

_____

Where or how did they meet?

_____

_____

_____

_____

_____

_____

_____

_____

_____

_____

What level of education did they have?

_____

_____

_____

_____

_____

_____

_____

_____

_____

_____

_____

What did they do for a living?

_____

_____

_____

_____

_____

_____

_____

_____

_____

Did they have any special opportunities given/offered to them?

_____

_____

_____

_____

_____

_____

_____

_____

_____

_____

Where did they live?

_____

_____

_____

_____

_____

_____

_____

_____

_____

What if any significant events were occurring in the world during

their lifetime?

_____

_____

_____

_____

_____

_____

_____

_____

_____

_____

What was the political environment like?

What made each of your parents "special" to you?

How would you describe their discipline or parenting style?

_____

_____

_____

_____

_____

_____

_____

_____

_____

What do you remember most vividly about each of them growing up as a child?

_____

_____

_____

_____

_____

_____

_____

Are your parents still living?

What was/is their health like?

What was each one's role in your family?

_____
_____
_____
_____
_____
_____
_____
_____
_____

Who was your biggest supporter in your family?

_____
_____
_____
_____
_____
_____
_____
_____
_____
_____
_____

What, if any, hobbies or special interests did/do they have?

_____

_____

_____

_____

_____

_____

_____

_____

What characteristic of his/her personality made him/her stand out?

_____

_____

_____

_____

_____

_____

_____

_____

_____

What is your relationship with your parents like today?

_____

_____

_____

_____

_____

_____

_____

_____

_____

_____

In what ways have your parents/upbringing influenced you the most?

_____

_____

_____

_____

_____

_____

_____

_____

_____

What one lesson did you learn from your mother that you carry with you today?

_____

_____

_____

_____

_____

_____

_____

_____

What one lesson did you learn from your father that you carry with you today?

_____

_____

_____

_____

_____

_____

_____

_____

Did your family have any silly sayings or jokes?

_____

_____

_____

_____

_____

_____

_____

_____

_____

Is there something that you wish you had asked or knew about your

parents?

_____

_____

_____

_____

_____

_____

_____

_____

_____

When and where were you born?

_____

_____

_____

_____

_____

_____

_____

_____

_____

How did your parents choose your name? Does it have any significant meaning?

_____

_____

_____

_____

_____

_____

_____

_____

_____

_____

Do you like your name?

_____

_____

_____

_____

_____

_____

_____

_____

_____

_____

What was your first home like?

_____

_____

_____

_____

_____

_____

_____

_____

_____

_____

Have you lived anywhere else? Outside of the country?

_____

_____

_____

_____

_____

_____

_____

_____

_____

If you went back there today, would it be just like your remembered it?

_____

_____

_____

_____

_____

_____

_____

_____

_____

Do you know of any interesting stories regarding your birth or your
mother's pregnancy?

_____

_____

_____

_____

_____

_____

_____

_____

_____

How many siblings do you have?

_____

_____

_____

_____

_____

_____

_____

_____

_____

_____

If you do not have siblings, how has being an only child shaped
your life and personality?

_____

_____

_____

_____

_____

_____

_____

_____

Where do you fall in the birth order of your family?

_____

_____

_____

_____

_____

_____

_____

_____

_____

_____

What did you typically argue about?

_____

_____

_____

_____

_____

_____

_____

_____

_____

How do you feel that your birth order shaped your personality?

_____

_____

_____

_____

_____

_____

_____

_____

_____

_____

How is your relationship with your siblings? Has it changed since you were children?

_____

_____

_____

_____

_____

_____

_____

_____

What is your earliest memory?

_____

_____

_____

_____

_____

_____

_____

_____

_____

Who were your playmates?

_____

_____

_____

_____

_____

_____

_____

_____

Do you remember the name of your first friend or any friends when
you were very young?

_____

_____

_____

_____

_____

_____

_____

_____

Were you bullied or picked on? Were you the bully?

_____
_____
_____
_____
_____
_____
_____
_____

Did you have any pets? What kind?

_____
_____
_____
_____
_____
_____
_____
_____
_____

Who was the most influential person in your life when you were young?

_____

_____

_____

_____

_____

_____

_____

_____

_____

_____

What did you do during school breaks/summertime?

_____

_____

_____

_____

_____

_____

_____

_____

_____

Can you describe a very memorable birthday?

_____

_____

_____

_____

_____

_____

_____

_____

_____

Did you have a nickname?

_____

_____

_____

_____

_____

_____

_____

_____

_____

_____

What was your bedtime/nighttime routine?

_____

_____

_____

_____

_____

_____

_____

_____

_____

_____

What were you afraid of?

_____

_____

_____

_____

_____

_____

_____

_____

_____

_____

_____

Did you have any imaginary friends?

_____

_____

_____

_____

_____

_____

_____

_____

_____

Can you remember the gift you received as a child that meant the
most to you? Why?

_____

_____

_____

_____

_____

_____

_____

_____

_____

_____

Did your family take any vacations that you can remember at that young age?

_____

_____

_____

_____

_____

_____

_____

_____

Do you have any funny or interesting stories about your toddler/ elementary school years?

_____

_____

_____

_____

_____

_____

_____

_____

Do you have an object that you treasure from your childhood?

_____

_____

_____

_____

_____

_____

_____

_____

_____

Would you say that you had a happy, fulfilled childhood?

_____

_____

_____

_____

_____

_____

_____

_____

_____

Which one of your parents do you most resemble or are you most like?

_____

_____

_____

_____

_____

_____

_____

_____

_____

_____

What are you most proud of as a child?

_____

_____

_____

_____

_____

_____

_____

_____

_____

_____

_____

Did you enjoy school?

_____
_____
_____
_____
_____
_____
_____
_____
_____
_____

What was your favorite subject?

_____
_____
_____
_____
_____
_____
_____
_____
_____
_____

What did you like most about school? Least about school?

_____
_____
_____
_____
_____
_____
_____
_____
_____

Was learning to read/write difficult or easy for you?

_____
_____
_____
_____
_____
_____
_____
_____

Do you remember anything that your teachers and/or parents said about you when you were young?

_____

_____

_____

_____

_____

_____

_____

_____

_____

What did you want to be when you grew up?

_____

_____

_____

_____

_____

_____

_____

_____

_____

_____

Did you play any sports?

_____

_____

_____

_____

_____

_____

_____

_____

_____

Did you have a part-time job? Where was it?

_____

_____

_____

_____

_____

_____

_____

_____

_____

_____

How did you spend/save any money that you earned?

_____

_____

_____

_____

_____

_____

_____

_____

_____

What did you learn about money as a child that helped/hurt your
financial life as an adult?

_____

_____

_____

_____

_____

_____

_____

_____

_____

What was your first car?

_____

_____

_____

_____

_____

_____

_____

_____

_____

_____

How would you describe yourself academically?

_____

_____

_____

_____

_____

_____

_____

_____

_____

_____

Did you have a favorite teacher? One that may have influenced you?

_____

_____

_____

_____

_____

_____

_____

_____

_____

What did you do outside of school? Hobbies?

_____

_____

_____

_____

_____

_____

_____

_____

_____

What music/dance/group was popular when you were in high school?

_____

_____

_____

_____

_____

_____

_____

_____

_____

_____

How would you describe yourself socially in high school?

_____

_____

_____

_____

_____

_____

_____

_____

_____

_____

Can you describe a fond memory from high school?

_____

_____

_____

_____

_____

_____

_____

_____

Did you have someone you admired or inspired you in high school?

_____

_____

_____

_____

_____

_____

_____

_____

_____

_____

Did you participate in any volunteer activities?

_____

_____

_____

_____

_____

_____

_____

_____

_____

_____

What did you learn about yourself during high school?

_____

_____

_____

_____

_____

_____

_____

_____

_____

_____

Do you think your high school education prepared you for college and/ or life after high school?

_____
_____
_____
_____
_____
_____
_____
_____
_____
_____

Have you remained in contact with anyone from high school?

_____
_____
_____
_____
_____
_____
_____
_____
_____
_____

Did you attend your high school 5-year, 10-year reunions?

_____

_____

_____

_____

_____

_____

_____

_____

_____

_____

Do you recall any significant local/global events that occurred during

this time?

_____

_____

_____

_____

_____

_____

_____

_____

_____

_____

What do you want to tell your 15-year old self?

Did you attend college? Trade school? Was there a particular event or circumstance surrounding your high school graduation?

_____

_____

_____

_____

_____

_____

_____

_____

_____

_____

If you attended college, which one? Did you live there or commute?

_____

_____

_____

_____

_____

_____

_____

_____

_____

_____

Why did you decide to attend college?

_____

_____

_____

_____

_____

_____

_____

_____

_____

_____

What did you study and why?

_____

_____

_____

_____

_____

_____

_____

_____

_____

_____

Did you have a roommate/close friend?

_____

_____

_____

_____

_____

_____

_____

_____

Did this friend influence you, positively/negatively?

_____

_____

_____

_____

_____

_____

_____

_____

Are you satisfied with the education you received?

_____
_____
_____
_____
_____
_____
_____
_____
_____
_____

If you had the option of doing it all over again, would you go down the same academic path?

_____
_____
_____
_____
_____
_____
_____
_____
_____
_____
_____

Can you describe a very memorable moment in college?

_____

_____

_____

_____

_____

_____

_____

_____

_____

_____

Did you serve in the military? When? Where? What were your duties?

_____

_____

_____

_____

_____

_____

_____

_____

_____

_____

_____

Why did you choose to enlist in the military?

_____

_____

_____

_____

_____

_____

_____

_____

_____

_____

How did you tell your family/friends of your decision to enlist?

_____

_____

_____

_____

_____

_____

_____

_____

_____

How did your military service impact your life?

_____

_____

_____

_____

_____

_____

_____

_____

_____

_____

Did anything significant happen in your life to guide you down this particular path towards a career?

_____

_____

_____

_____

_____

_____

_____

_____

_____

Did you have a role model?

_____

_____

_____

_____

_____

_____

_____

_____

_____

_____

Did you participate in any extra-curricular activities?

_____

_____

_____

_____

_____

_____

_____

_____

_____

_____

_____

Do you think your college education prepared you for the real world?

_____

_____

_____

_____

_____

_____

_____

_____

_____

_____

Did you form any life-long relationships during this time?

_____

_____

_____

_____

_____

_____

_____

_____

_____

_____

_____

Did you remain in contact with high school/home friends while you
were in college?

What was your first job?

When was the moment you felt truly grown up?

How did you obtain your first job? Was it in your field of study?

_____

_____

_____

_____

_____

_____

_____

_____

How much was your first paycheck?

_____

_____

_____

_____

_____

_____

_____

_____

_____

Did it meet your expectations of what you envisioned from your
college experience?

_____

_____

_____

_____

_____

_____

_____

_____

_____

How would you describe your work ethic?

_____

_____

_____

_____

_____

_____

_____

_____

_____

How would you describe your ideal job/career?

_____

_____

_____

_____

_____

_____

_____

_____

_____

Have you experienced the "ideal job"?

_____

_____

_____

_____

_____

_____

_____

_____

_____

_____

Did you have a mentor or someone who influenced you?

_____

_____

_____

_____

_____

_____

_____

_____

_____

_____

How did this person impact your life/career?

_____

_____

_____

_____

_____

_____

_____

_____

_____

_____

What other jobs have you had?

_____

_____

_____

_____

_____

_____

_____

_____

_____

Do you enjoy your line of work? Does your job bring you personal
satisfaction?

_____

_____

_____

_____

_____

_____

_____

_____

_____

What do you enjoy doing outside of work? Hobbies?

_____

_____

_____

_____

_____

_____

_____

_____

_____

_____

Did you ever work more than one job?

_____

_____

_____

_____

_____

_____

_____

_____

_____

_____

What was/is your ultimate career goal?

_____

_____

_____

_____

_____

_____

_____

_____

_____

_____

How do you define "success"?

_____

_____

_____

_____

_____

_____

_____

_____

_____

_____

_____

Have you thought about retirement?

_____

_____

_____

_____

_____

_____

_____

_____

_____

How do/did you envision your life after leaving the working world?

_____

_____

_____

_____

_____

_____

_____

_____

_____

_____

How has/will retirement change your life in terms of activities you had not done previously?

_____

_____

_____

_____

_____

_____

_____

_____

Has your job/career brought you all the rewards you expected and deserve? What are they?

_____

_____

_____

_____

_____

_____

_____

_____

Do you feel valued and appreciated? Is this something that is important to you?

_____

_____

_____

_____

_____

_____

_____

_____

_____

If you could change anything about your career choice, what would that one thing be?

_____

_____

_____

_____

_____

_____

_____

_____

If you are/did not work in your original career choice, what did you do and why?

_____

_____

_____

_____

_____

_____

_____

_____

What has been your greatest challenge in terms of your career?

_____

_____

_____

_____

_____

_____

_____

_____

_____

WORK LIFE

Do you participate in any volunteer activities?

_____
_____
_____
_____
_____
_____
_____
_____
_____

Do you have any regrets about your job or career choices?

_____
_____
_____
_____
_____
_____
_____
_____
_____
_____

If you hit the lottery, what is the first thing you would do?

Who was your first love?

_____

_____

_____

_____

_____

_____

_____

_____

_____

_____

Are you married or in a relationship?

_____

_____

_____

_____

_____

_____

_____

_____

_____

_____

_____

Where did you meet your spouse or significant other?

How long have you been together?

What advice would you give your children about marriage or relationships?

_____

_____

_____

_____

_____

_____

_____

_____

_____

Is there anything special or significant about your relationship?

_____

_____

_____

_____

_____

_____

_____

_____

_____

What would you say is the more important characteristic of your relationship?

_____

_____

_____

_____

_____

_____

_____

What kinds of things do you disagree about?

_____

_____

_____

_____

_____

_____

_____

_____

_____

What does your spouse do for a living?

_____

_____

_____

_____

_____

_____

_____

_____

_____

How would you describe your marriage?

_____

_____

_____

_____

_____

_____

_____

_____

_____

_____

Is there something that you used to do together that you no longer do?

_____

_____

_____

_____

_____

_____

_____

_____

What do you enjoy doing together with your spouse?

_____

_____

_____

_____

_____

_____

_____

_____

Can you name something that you admire in your spouse?

_____

_____

_____

_____

_____

_____

_____

_____

_____

If you are not married, have you ever been? Will you provide some
details about the marriage?

_____

_____

_____

_____

_____

_____

_____

_____

_____

If you have never been, what qualities do you look for in a partner?

_____

_____

_____

_____

_____

_____

_____

_____

_____

Who is your best friend and why?

_____

_____

_____

_____

_____

_____

_____

_____

_____

_____

How has this person been involved with your life?

_____

_____

_____

_____

_____

_____

_____

_____

_____

_____

What do you share with your best friend that you would not tell
your spouse?

_____

_____

_____

_____

_____

_____

_____

_____

_____

What characteristic do you value in others?

Do you have children? How old? Gender?

_____

_____

_____

_____

_____

_____

_____

_____

_____

How were you changed with the birth of each of your children?

_____

_____

_____

_____

_____

_____

_____

_____

_____

_____

What is your goal as a parent?

_____

_____

_____

_____

_____

_____

_____

_____

What is your greatest dream/expectation for your children?

_____

_____

_____

_____

_____

_____

_____

_____

_____

How would your children describe you as a parent? Is this the same or different to how you would describe yourself as a parent?

_____

_____

_____

_____

_____

_____

_____

_____

_____

Is there anything in your parenting style that you do specifically because it is different than how you were raised?

_____

_____

_____

_____

_____

_____

_____

_____

_____

What role do you play in your home?

_____

_____

_____

_____

_____

_____

_____

_____

If you do not have children, why/why not?

_____

_____

_____

_____

_____

_____

_____

_____

What little white lie about your past have you told your children?

What good quality in you do you hope to pass on to your children?

What bad quality in you do you hope to not pass on to your children?

_____

_____

_____

_____

_____

_____

_____

_____

What is one family tradition that you hope to pass on to your children or grandchildren?

_____

_____

_____

_____

_____

_____

_____

_____

How is your family unique?

_____

_____

_____

_____

_____

_____

_____

_____

_____

_____

What do you think is the most difficult thing about raising children?

_____

_____

_____

_____

_____

_____

_____

_____

_____

_____

What are you passionate about?

_____

_____

_____

_____

_____

_____

_____

_____

_____

What makes you want to get out of bed every day?

_____

_____

_____

_____

_____

_____

_____

_____

_____

How would you define happiness?

_____

_____

_____

_____

_____

_____

_____

_____

_____

_____

_____

What accomplishment are you most proud of?

_____

_____

_____

_____

_____

_____

_____

_____

_____

_____

_____

What has been your greatest challenge in life?

_____
_____
_____
_____
_____
_____
_____
_____
_____

How do you want to be remembered?

_____
_____
_____
_____
_____
_____
_____
_____
_____
_____
_____

What do you hope to leave as your Legacy?

_____

_____

_____

_____

_____

_____

_____

_____

_____

What is your greatest fear?

_____

_____

_____

_____

_____

_____

_____

_____

_____

_____

What is the scariest thing that has ever happened to you?

_____

_____

_____

_____

_____

_____

_____

_____

_____

What is your favorite book and why?

_____

_____

_____

_____

_____

_____

_____

_____

_____

_____

Can you explain your most embarrassing moment?

_____
_____
_____
_____
_____
_____
_____
_____
_____

If you could go back in time and change one moment or event, what would it be and why?

_____
_____
_____
_____
_____
_____
_____
_____

Have you traveled outside of your home country? Do you prefer to visit/learn about local cultures or do you prefer tourist attractions?

_____

_____

_____

_____

_____

_____

_____

_____

What is your favorite food?

_____

_____

_____

_____

_____

_____

_____

_____

_____

_____

Do you have any bad habits?

_____

_____

_____

_____

_____

_____

_____

_____

_____

_____

What is your biggest pet peeve?

_____

_____

_____

_____

_____

_____

_____

_____

_____

If you had more time in your day, what would you do?

_____

_____

_____

_____

_____

_____

_____

_____

_____

Is there anything missing in your life?

_____

_____

_____

_____

_____

_____

_____

_____

_____

_____

What characteristic in others is the most annoying to you?

_____

_____

_____

_____

_____

_____

_____

_____

_____

Do you have anything that you regret doing/not doing?

_____

_____

_____

_____

_____

_____

_____

_____

_____

Have you experienced the death of a loved one? If so, who? How did it impact your life?

_____

_____

_____

_____

_____

_____

_____

Can you describe something that has significantly changed the trajectory of your life?

_____

_____

_____

_____

_____

_____

_____

_____

How have you made an impact on someone, besides your family/
relatives, life?

What one quality makes YOU different from anyone else?

What is one thing that you would change about yourself if you could?

What main lesson have you learned in life?

Do you have a personal mantra? Rule to live by?

_____

_____

_____

_____

_____

_____

_____

_____

_____

_____

What one message do you want to relay to your audience?

_____

_____

_____

_____

_____

_____

_____

_____

_____

_____

_____

If you could go back in time, what time period would you want to live in/have been born in?

_____

_____

_____

_____

_____

_____

_____

_____

_____

What do you believe is/was your life's purpose?

_____

_____

_____

_____

_____

_____

_____

_____

_____

_____

_____

What have you done in your life that was outside of your comfort zone?

_____

_____

_____

_____

_____

_____

_____

_____

_____

_____

What do you wish you had done differently?

_____

_____

_____

_____

_____

_____

_____

_____

_____

_____

What would you say was the best time period of your life?

_____

_____

_____

_____

_____

_____

_____

_____

_____

Can you define the worst time in your life?

_____

_____

_____

_____

_____

_____

_____

_____

_____

Can you identify a defining moment or turning point in your life?

_____

_____

_____

_____

_____

_____

_____

_____

_____

How has your life experience prepared you for your career/book/next phase of life?

_____

_____

_____

_____

_____

_____

_____

_____

Can you define the lowest point in your life?

Have you ever been someone's "solution"?

Do you have a secret that you have never told anyone before?

_____

_____

_____

_____

_____

_____

_____

_____

_____

_____

_____

Who would you consider your hero?

_____

_____

_____

_____

_____

_____

_____

_____

_____

_____

_____

What famous quote would you say most defines you?

_____

_____

_____

_____

_____

_____

_____

_____

_____

What things make you laugh? Cry?

_____

_____

_____

_____

_____

_____

_____

_____

_____

Are there any additional events that helped to shape who you have become? Positive? Negative?

Are there any contradictions or ironies about your life?

_____

_____

_____

_____

_____

_____

_____

_____

_____

What tough questions do you ask yourself every day?

_____

_____

_____

_____

_____

_____

_____

_____

_____

_____

Do you question your own existence, survival or resilience?

_____

_____

_____

_____

_____

_____

_____

_____

_____

_____

Do you have a "Bucket List" of things that you would like to accomplish/
do in your life?

_____

_____

_____

_____

_____

_____

_____

_____

_____

What one word would your friends use to describe you?

What is something that you are most grateful for?

Where do you see yourself in the next 10 years? 20 years?

_____
_____
_____
_____
_____
_____
_____
_____
_____
_____

What do you value most in your life? Your family?

_____
_____
_____
_____
_____
_____
_____
_____
_____
_____

How have the things that are important to you changed over the years?

Do you have any religious affiliation?

_____

_____

_____

_____

_____

_____

_____

_____

_____

_____

How do you define spirituality?

_____

_____

_____

_____

_____

_____

_____

_____

_____

_____

What has most impacted your belief system?

_____

_____

_____

_____

_____

_____

_____

_____

_____

_____

If you believe in God, do you believe He has a plan for your life?

_____

_____

_____

_____

_____

_____

_____

_____

_____

_____

How does religion impact your life?

_____

_____

_____

_____

_____

_____

_____

_____

_____

_____

_____

Have your religious beliefs changed since you were young?

_____

_____

_____

_____

_____

_____

_____

_____

_____

_____

_____

Was religion important in your family?

_____

_____

_____

_____

_____

_____

_____

_____

_____

What do you think happens after you die?

_____

_____

_____

_____

_____

_____

_____

_____

_____

_____

Do you think you can forgive someone from your past who has harmed or wronged you in life?

_____

_____

_____

_____

_____

_____

_____

_____

_____

Who would you like to see again if you could?

_____

_____

_____

_____

_____

_____

_____

_____

_____

_____

When you meet God, do you have anything you would like to ask Him?

What do you think happens after you die?

NOTES

NOTES

NOTES

NOTES

ADDITIONAL NOTES

NOTES

Sign Up to OneFam

At OneFam we aim to make family history available to everyone. We would like to invite you to become a member of OneFam community and enjoy exclusive benefits. With already over 25,000 users worldwide, we promise you'll be in good company.

- 50% off your next journal purchases
- Access to free family tree software
- Birthday gifts
- Free shipping offers
- First dibs on sales
- & more...

To subscribe, simply visit our website at:

https://www.onefam.com/subscribe/

ONE FAM

Create Your Family Free

Get started with your free online family tree in minutes. Simply sign up, add your parents, siblings, children, grandparents and other family members.

- Preserve Images, Videos, Audio, Stories & Events
- Invite & Connect with Family Members
- Create and Share Family History
- Available on Web, Mobile and Ipad

ONE FAM
www.onefam.com

More Great Journals

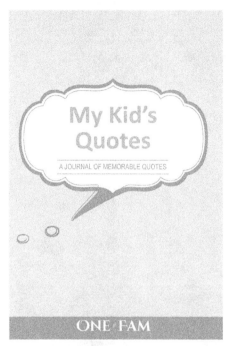

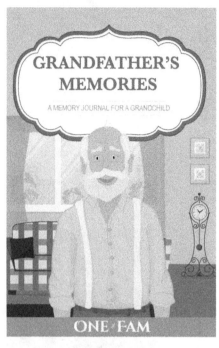

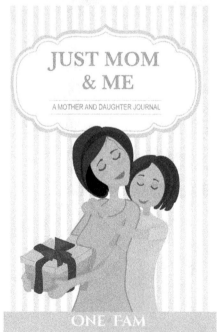

Visit Onefam.com for our full range

More Great Journals

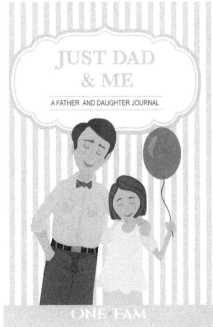

Visit Onefam.com for our full range

CPSIA information can be obtained
at www.ICGtesting.com
Printed in the USA
BVHW020152020523
663422BV00009B/198

9 781913 366315